AROMATHERAPY
THE PREGNANCY BOOK

by Jennie Supper RM RN MGCP

Published by
Amberwood Publishing Ltd
Guildford, England

PLANTLIFE

The Natural History Museum, Cromwell Road, London SW7 5BD

Registered Charity No. 328576

Amberwood Publishing supports the Plantlife Charity,
Britain's only charity exclusively dedicated to saving wild plants.

ISBN 1 899308-20-2

Cover production by Howland Northover

Printed in Great Britain

CONTENTS

About the Author

Jennie Supper is a registered nurse and a registered midwife. For the last 25 years she has worked as a community midwife in Reading. In 1995 she qualified as an aromatherapist. At the moment she is involved in putting together a policy for the use of aromatherapy for the hospital trust. Over the last few years there have been an increasing number of women wanting to use alternative methods of pain relief for labour and aromatherapy has proved beneficial for many.

For Adam, Mikki and Ben.
And for Alex without whom
this book wouldn't have been written.

Illustrations and Cover design by

PETER READ

GRAPHIC DESIGNER · ILLUSTRATOR
Tredavoe, Newlyn, Penzance, Cornwall, TR20 8TW.

...COMPUTERS CAN'T DO WHAT I DO! ...

Note to Reader

Whilst the author has made every effort to ensure that the contents of this book are accurate in every particular, it is not intended to be regarded as a substitute for professional medical advice under treatment. Readers are urged to give careful consideration to any difficulties which they may be experiencing with their own health and to consult their General Practitioner if uncertain as to its cause or nature. Neither the author nor the publisher can accept any legal responsibility for any health problem which results from use of the self-help methods described.

Foreword

I have been a practising GP for 22 years, and over this time, have seen the changes in childbirth technique from the high-tech approach to a more gentle, non-invasive form of pregnancy and delivery in non-threatening conditions.

Along with this trend, is the recognition that holistic therapies can be used to benefit and alleviate the miseries of the human condition. Homeopathy, herbal medicine and aromatherapy techniques have been used through the ages and are now being taken seriously by the medical profession. They have been shown to have many benefits when used properly with none of the side effects experienced with conventional medicines. No wonder then, that in the most natural and important function any woman can perform – that of giving birth to a child, there is a quest for gentle, pleasurable and non-toxic aids.

This carefully thought-out little book fills just that niche. Aromatherapeutic techniques when carefully applied, certainly have a very beneficial effect upon every aspect of pregnancy and birth. Jennie Supper has been a senior practising midwife for many years, and is now a qualified aromatherapist very skilled in her field. She has appreciated the benefits for her patients in using aromatherapy, and now hopes to pass on these tips and techniques to all pregnant women. This book is unique in concentrating on all aspects of pregnancy and childbirth, and for any woman wishing to make this time of her life as gentle, natural and memorable as possible, it is a *must*. Now read on . . .

Dr Susan E Williams

1 | Introduction to Aromatherapy

History of Aromatherapy

Man first discovered aromatherapy when he used plants and twigs to fuel his fires. He found that some plants made him feel happy, some made him relaxed, and some cured certain ailments.

The Chinese knowledge of oils is thought to have reached the west via the Greeks and the Romans.

The Egyptians used herbs for suppositories and medicines. Herbs were also used in the treatment of burns. Frankincense was found in the tombs

...THE CHINESE KNOWLEDGE OF OILS IS THOUGHT TO HAVE REACHED THE WEST VIA THE GREEKS AND THE ROMANS...

of some mummies. However they had not yet discovered how to distil the oils. In documents dating from 1000 BC it was discovered that honey, qualqint and acacia were used for contraception. Coriander was used for cooking.

The Romans acquired their knowledge from the Greeks. Hippocrates believed 'the daily use of aromatherapy oils and a daily massage is the way to health'. Greek soldiers carried myrrh into battle to dress their wounds.

The Romans contributed to Britain's flora by introducing different plants and herbs to the countryside e.g. parsley and fennel. Galen was the physician to the emperor Marcus Aurelius. He treated the gladiators with aromatic herbs and wines. It has been recorded that not one of the gladiators treated by Galen died of his wounds.

Avicenna was a gifted scholar, physician and philosopher. He lived in Persia (980-1037AD). Avicenna was said to have refined the distillation process of oils and to have produced purer oils. He left valuable records of some 800 plants. The Persians valued flower water from distilling orange

... GREEK SOLDIERS CARRIED MYRRH INTO BATTLE TO DRESS THEIR WOUNDS ...

blossom and roses. They used them as remedies for sickness as well as for cosmetics.

The Jews, when they began their exodus from Egypt (around 1280 BC) took precious oils for use in their flight from the Pharoah. They were used to anoint the priest with 'sweet incense and briar' (Exodus XXV 1-9). In the Songs of Solomon we see reference to valuable sources of oils.

In the New Testament, in the parable, the Good Samaritan treated the wounds of the traveller who had been attacked by thieves with wine and oil. As well as gold the three wise men brought Jesus frankincense and myrrh.

The first recorded use of essential oils in Britain was in the 13th century AD. The perfumed glove makers seemed to be protected from the plague because essential oils they used appeared to improve their immunity. There was no protection for others. Gentlemen carried posies of lavender and herbs to protect them from the awful smells and disease. Children were encouraged to wear lavender pouches around their necks as a protection against infections. Hygiene was non-existent. It is said, Queen Elizabeth I took a bath every six months whether she needed it or not. As the heavily bejewelled clothes were extremely difficult to launder the pomanders were probably essential to make everyday life bearable.

As the manufacture of essential oils increased they became widely used as medicines, antiseptics and perfumes. In the 19th century less expensive copies were made but the cheaper oils did not seem to have the same therapeutic properties. These cheaper imitations almost ended the therapeutic use of essential oils.

Rene Maurice Gattefosse, a French chemist coined the word 'aromatherapy'. He accidentally burnt his arm on a Bunsen burner. He then plunged his arm into a container of Lavender oil. This relieved the pain and the burn healed quickly without scarring. Gattefosse discovered the properties of other essential oils and used them in the treatment of wounded soldiers in the First World War.

Gatefosse's work was carried on by Jean Valnet, another French chemist, who treated sick and wounded soldiers during the Second World War. Valnet also claimed success in treating cancer, tuberculosis and other serious illnesses.

Marguerite Mauray introduced aromatherapy to this country. She was a French beautician and biochemist who extended its use into beauty products.

The Australian Aborigines still burn eucalyptus as a form of purification ritual to fumigate against illness.

The Advantages of Aromatherapy

Aromatherapy is a gentle and holistic therapy. (It works on mind, body and spirit). Its aims are not only to relieve and eliminate health problems but the prevention of disease and the promotion of healthy living. In modern medicine plants are used when the active chemicals are isolated which may be the reason some have side effects.

The Extraction of Oils

There are five methods for the extraction of essential oils: Distillation; Enfleurage; Maceration; Expression; Solvent extraction.

... AROMATHERAPY IS A GENTLE AND HOLISTIC THERAPY — IT WORKS ON MIND, BODY AND SPIRIT ...

Distillation

This is the oldest and most widely used method of separating the oil from the plant. The plant is heated with water, or steam, or both in a still and the vapour produced is channelled in a condenser. The resulting liquid is a mixture of oil and water with the oil floating on top (or if the oil is heavier sinking to the bottom). The oil can then be drawn off.

Enfleurage

This method is used for plants that carry on producing essential oils after harvesting. Purified fat is spread onto a sheet of glass, this being covered by a layer of freshly picked flowers. After about twenty-four hours the flowers will have given up their oil to the fat. The flowers are then shaken off and a fresh layer is put on. This process may continue for up to seventy days, depending on the quality of the harvest and the flowers involved. When the fat has been completely saturated with the perfume (this is called the pomade) it is washed in alcohol while being mechanically agitated. The oils are soluble in the alcohol. The alcohol is then evaporated off, leaving the essential oil.

Maceration

This method is for plants which stop producing oils after harvesting. The plants are plunged into hot fat. The hot fat then penetrates their cells. The flowers are then removed by straining or in a centrifuge and more flowers

...THE OLDEST AND MOST WIDELY USED METHOD OF SEPARATING THE OIL FROM THE PLANT...

are added. This may be repeated up to fifteen times, depending on the plants or the harvest. The resulting pomade is then washed and mixed with alcohol. The oils are soluble in the alcohol, which is then evaporated, leaving the essential oil.

Expression
This method of extraction is for citrus fruits (orange, lemon, grapefruit, tangerine and mandarin). The oil is hand squeezed from the rind onto a sponge. When the sponge becomes saturated the oil is pressed out of it into a container (Sponge process). This is now performed by machine.

Solvent Extraction
The flowers or other parts of the plant are placed in a vessel and covered with the solvent. The mixture is slowly heated, during which process the aromatic oils are released from the plant. This is then filtered resulting in a dark coloured paste known as concrete. The concrete is then mixed with alcohol and chilled. The aromatic oils are then transferred to the alcohol leaving insoluble wax as a residue. The solution is then filtered and the alcohol evaporated. The paste after being mixed with the alcohol is known as the absolute.

Base Oils or Carrier Oils
A base oil or carrier oil can be any odourless vegetable oil. Pure essential oils are too concentrated to be put directly onto the skin, and apart from a couple of exceptions should never be used neat. They should always be diluted in the correct proportions before use, since if used too concentrated they may do more harm than good. The oils should be diluted in a base carrier oil. These base carrier oils should be pure and of a good quality. Baby oil, which is a mineral oil (petroleum based) should never be used as it does not penetrate the skin and restricts the passage of essential oils into the body through the skin. Therefore the benefits of the oils are not reaped. The carrier oils should not have been chemically processed.

Sweet Almond Oil
This oil is an excellent carrier and is good for all skin types. Please note, this oil is not recommended if allergic to nuts

Corn Oil

This oil is good for all skin types. It has a good content of minerals and protein. It is soothing and good for itchy and irritated skin.

Grape Seed Oil

This oil is inexpensive and good for all skin types. It is easily absorbed but unfortunately can stain.

Sunflower Oil

This oil is similar to Sweet Almond Oil.

Dilution of Essential Oils

1%   – 1 drop per 5ml (1 teaspoonful) of carrier oil
2%   – 12 drops per 30ml container of carrier oil
2½% – 15 drops per 30ml container of carrier oil
       (Divide 30 by 2 = 15)
       Therefore for a 50ml container use 25 drops

...PURE ESSENTIAL OILS ARE TOO CONCENTRATED TO BE PUT DIRECTLY ONTO THE SKIN ...

If the oils are too concentrated (importance of correct use and dilution) they may have a reverse effect. It is advisable not to use essential oil therapy for prolonged periods without consulting a qualified aromatherapist.

Safety and the use of oil – some do's and don'ts

Never take essential oils orally. The oils are very toxic and if taken orally without supervision could have serious results.

Do not use essential oils neat as they are too concentrated (With the exception of Lavender and Tea Tree).

Do not use in the first three months of pregnancy.

Do not massage the abdomen during the first three months of pregnancy as it could cause a miscarriage.

Take care with sensitive skin.

Store away from children.

Keep away from the eyes.

Do not massage over recent scar tissue, fresh scars or wounds.

Be aware that some oils have contraindications.

Storage of Oils

Store the oil in a cool, dark cupboard away from the light and from children.

Do not decant the oils from their coloured bottles to clear or plastic bottles. Plastic bottles may perish and clear bottles allow the light to affect the oils.

Once diluted in a base oil the pure oil has a shelf life of three months, otherwise it has a shelf life of two to three years if kept in the correct conditions.

Citrus oils may only have a shelf life of one year because they tend to oxidise.

How to Use the Oils

Massage is the method chosen by the aromatherapist. Massage even without essential oil is a very powerful instrument. Touch itself is an unspoken means of communication. Massage nourishes the skin, is relaxing and it also helps with the absorption of the oils through the skin. Massage affects all the systems of the body. It has a physiological and psychological effect. The person receiving the massage must like the smell of the oil used. Do not use an oil that you don't like the smell of.

When not to massage

Over the abdomen in pregnancy.
Over varicose veins.
Over recent scar tissue.
Over rashes.
Over fresh bruising.
Over areas of inflammation.

...DO NOT USE AN OIL THAT YOU DO NOT LIKE THE SMELL OF...

When not to massage *(cont)*
Over the back if there are any acute or chronic conditions.
Over unrecognised lumps or bumps.
In serious medical conditions.
Over open wounds.
If on certain medication (consult doctor or midwife).
In cases of infection (bacterial, fungal or viral).
After recent surgery.
Over broken bones.
If there is a fever.
If in doubt always consult your doctor or midwife.

Baths. The Romans and the Egyptians had public baths and throughout history used them therapeutically and for pleasure. Hippocrates, a Greek who lived in the fifth century BC, said that 'the way to health was an aromatic bath and a scented massage every day'. What a joy!

This is the simplest and most enjoyable way of using the oils. Run a bath, and when it is full add eight to ten drops of your chosen diluted essential oil, swish it round and climb in. The essential oils should be mixed with two teaspoonsful of a base oil, e.g. sunflower oil first to avoid too much concentration on the skin, as some oils can be irritants. Instead of sunflower oil, top of the milk, cream or vodka can be used.

Sitz bath. This is useful for haemorrhoids, and painful perineii. Sprinkle six drops of pure essential oil (first diluted in a chosen teaspoonful of base oil) into a suitable bowl of warm water. Sit in the bowl for five to ten minutes. Lavender can be used neat.

Compresses. These are a very effective way to relieve pain.

Hot Compress. Fill a bowl with very hot water, and then add six drops of essential oil. Dip a folded piece of cotton, cotton wool or flannel into the bowl, squeeze it out and place on the affected area until it is cooled.

Cold Compresses are made the same way, but ice-cold water is used instead. They can reduce swelling.

... THE WAY TO HEALTH WAS AN AROMATIC BATH AND A SCENTED MASSAGE EVERY DAY...

... INSTEAD OF SUNFLOWER OIL - TOP OF THE MILK, CREAM OR VODKA CAN BE USED...

Vaporisers. An oil burner can be used, a diffuser, or a few drops of oil can be placed on a light bulb ring, or added to a bowl of water and placed on a radiator. A plant sprayer filled with water to which ten drops of essential oil has been added may also be used.

Internally. NEVER!

Neat application. Only two oils can be used neat: Lavender and Tea Tree, otherwise the oil should always be diluted in a carrier oil. (See Dilution instructions on page 15)

2 | Essential Oils

CHAMOMILE

EXTRACTION is by distillation of the heads of the flowers.

There are two types used: German Chamomile (*Matricaria recutica*) and Roman Chamomile (*Chamaemelum nobile*). German Chamomile contains more azulene. Azulene is not present in the fresh flower and is only formed in the distilling process. Azulene is an excellent anti-inflammatory agent.

Chamomile was called 'grand apple' by the ancient Greeks because of its smell. The Spaniards called it manzinilla, meaning 'little apple'. The Saxons supposed it to be one of the nine sacred herbs given by the god Woden. As it cured fevers, the Egyptians dedicated it to the sun. Other sources said that it was dedicated to the moon, because of its cooling effects.

Chamomile is also called the *plant physician* as it was thought to have kept other plants healthy. Planted next to a sickly plant, it will revive it, and insects tend to avoid Chamomile.

Chamomile's efficiency in treating female disorders gave rise to the German name which, when translated, means *mother herb*. It was spread on floors in houses because of its sweet smell when trodden on, and its insect-repellent qualities.

Chamomile is known as the children's oil as it is so gentle and safe.

Uses: Sensitive skin, cracked skin, dyspepsia, colic, indigestion, nausea, headaches, nervous tension, stress, insomnia.

Conjunctivitis? Then use Chamomile tea bags soaked in boiling water, cooled and rested over the eyes.

Caution: Do not use in the first three months of pregnancy.

CINNAMON (*Cinnamonium zeylancium*)

EXTRACTION is by water and steam distillation from either the dried inner bark or the leaves and twigs.

For thousands of years Cinnamon has been used and valued for a wide range of conditions including digestive and menstrual disorders. It was one of the spices mentioned in the Bible and it was brought to Europe in the 17th century by the Portuguese who invaded Sri Lanka. Cinnamon bark appears to have been collected from wild Cinnamon tree plants towards the end of the 13th century AD. After the invasion of the Portuguese in 1536 exportation became more regular. In 1770 the cultivation was successfully carried out by the Dutch who tried hard to control the supply of Cinnamon and therefore the price. Soon the British gained control of the island. The Chinese make use of their native Cinnamon, using both the bark and the twigs. (The bark for the torso and the twigs for the fingers and the toes). References to aromatic Cinnamon bark are abundant in the Old Testament.

Cinnamon comes from the inner bark of the new shoots. Every two years it is harvested and sold as Cinnamon sticks. Cinnamon bark and leaf oil is used in flavouring for food and drinks, including coca cola.

Uses: Only during labour. It helps with pain relief and produces efficient contractions.

Cautions: Only use the leaf oil, as bark oil is a dermal irritant and a sensitiser. Do not use during pregnancy as it can cause premature labour.

CLARY SAGE (*Salvia sclaria*)

EXTRACTION is by steam distillation from the flowers and the stems.

This plant was highly esteemed during the middle ages but is less used now. Sclaria came from the Greek "skleria" meaning hard, this refers to the white blue flowers that end in a hard blue part. It also derives from the Latin "clarius" meaning clear as it was also used to clear the mucous from the eyes.

This oil is a good tonic for the womb and is particularly useful for uterine problems. It helps with labour as it aids relaxation and can help prevent postnatal depression.

Uses: High blood pressure, muscular aches and pains, during labour, depression, stress. It helps during labour and may help prevent postnatal depression. During labour it produces efficient contractions – it helps with pain relief.

Cautions: Do not use in pregnancy. Do not use when drinking alcohol as it can enhance the action of the alcohol, cause nightmares or as with some drugs cause a 'bad trip', or headaches.

CYPRESS (*Cupressus sempervirens*)

EXTRACTION is by steam distillation from the needles and twigs.

Cypress was planted by the Romans in their burial grounds. Pluto, the god of the underworld was supposed to have planted one by his palace. As cypress wood does not easily decay the Greeks used to carve their gods in it. The Egyptians used it for their sarcophagi and for medicines. Cypress was dedicated to the gods of death and the underworld by both the Romans and the Greeks.

The Chinese consider Cypress nuts very nutritious, and beneficial for the liver, respiration, and checking excess perspiration. The Tibetans use Cypress as a purification incense.

Uses: Oedema, poor circulation, varicose veins, haemmorrhoids.

EUCALYPTUS (*Eucalyptus globulus var globulus*)

EXTRACTION is by steam distillation of the leaves and twigs.

This tree is native to Australia and Tasmania but has been cultivated in Southern Europe and Africa. It was planted to dry up marshy areas and thus eradicate the malaria mosquito.

Eucalyptus oil is very warming and is especially good for treating chest complaints and fevers. It is anti bacterial and anti viral. Eucalyptus oil is used in many vapour rubs.

The Aborigines burn the leaves to relieve fevers and bind the leaves around wounds to heal them and prevent infections.

The dried leaves are smoked as cigarettes for the treatment of asthma.

Uses: Wounds, burns, insect repellent, asthma, flu, bronchitis.

Caution: Not under any circumstance to be taken orally.

... THE DRIED LEAVES ARE SMOKED AS CIGARETTES FOR THE TREATMENT OF ASTHMA ...

FENNEL (*Foeniculum vulgare*)

EXTRACTION is by steam distillation. Sweet Fennel oil is obtained by distilling the crushed seeds.

Fennel imitates the action of oestrogen. Culpeper says that is 'the herb of Mercury under Virgo,' and says, 'it is good to provoke the wind. The leaves or seeds are boiled in barley water and drank, and are good for nursing mothers to increase their milk, and make it more wholesome for the child.' Culpeper also says, 'It assists also to bring down the courses, and cleanse the parts after delivery.'

FENNEL...IN MEDIEVAL TIMES, IT WAS HUNG OVER DOORS TO KEEP WITCHES AWAY...

In experiments with goats, it was found to increase the quality of, and the fat in their milk. Fennel was also used in gripe water.

Highly respected as a food and medicine in ancient Greece and Rome, it was thought to have magical powers. In Medieval times, it was hung over doors to keep away witches. The Romans believed that serpents sucked the fennel to improve their eyesight. Fennel was also regarded as an early slimming aid. Its Greek name was 'marathion', which means 'to grow slim', probably because it gave a feeling of fullness.

The fennel fruit was used by the ancient Romans. The succulent fruits are also used as a vegetable by the Italians. The Emperor Charlemagne cultivated this plant in Central Europe.

Uses: Bruises, insufficient milk production in nursing mothers, colic, constipation, flatulence.

Caution: Use of this oil should be avoided during pregnancy, and by epileptics. Fennel oil should only be used in the post natal period and not during pregnancy.

FRANKINCENSE (*Boswelli carteri*)
EXTRACTION by steam distillation from selected oleo gum resin.

Frankincense is a gum resin, obtained from the *Boswelli carteri*. Frankincense has been burned in temples and on altars since history began. It has meditative qualities, and has the ability to slow down and deepen the breath. It also produces feelings of tranquility and calm.

Frankincense was one of the most costly of all the substances in the ancient world, and was one of the gifts brought by the Three Wise Men to Jesus. The Hebrews and Egyptians spent vast amounts of money importing from the Phoenicians. In fact, it was far more valuable than gold. Frankincense was also used for embalming.

The name 'frankincense' is derived from the French, and means 'real incense'.

Frankincense is an uterine tonic, and can be used in baths. It is safe to use in pregnancy, and is very useful for treating the genito-urinary tract.

Uses: Cystitis, anxiety, stress.

GERANIUM (*Pelargonium graveolens*)
EXTRACTION is by steam distillation from the leaves, stalks and flowers.

Culpeper describes this plant as 'being under the influence of Venus'.

Geranium oil is a mild analgesic and sedative. It is used when pain is more nervous than physical. It works on the adrenal cortex, and therefore helps to regulate and balance the hormones. It is also astringent.

Geranium was once regarded as a great healing plant, and was often used for healing wounds. It used to be planted around cottages, to keep evil spirits at bay.

It is diuretic, and stimulates the lymphatic system. Also, it is a tonic for the circulatory system. Geranium helps to guard against fluid retention, and is therefore good for swollen ankles. Geranium is said to be helpful with 'inflammation and congestion of the breast', and therefore it is good for engorgement of the breasts. It is also good for depression, haemorrhoids and stretch marks.

Geranium leaves put on nipples, furry side in will help heal cracked nipples. They are the correct shape and size. They may tingle. In case of itching and irritation (which is rare) remove them at once.

Uses: Bruises, cuts, haemorrhoids, cellulitis, breast engorgement, oedema, nervous tension and stress.

Caution: Geranium oil may cause some irritation to sensitive skin.

... GERANIUM LEAVES PUT ON NIPPLES, FURRY SIDE IN WILL HELP HEAL CRACKED NIPPLES...

JASMINE (*Jasminum officinale*)

EXTRACTION is produced by solvent extraction (concrete). An absolute is produced from separation with alcohol.

Jasmine is also known as 'king of oils'. This is also one of the best oils for childbirth, but is also one of the most expensive, as a large number of flowers is required to produce a relatively small amount of oil. Cheaper Jasmine oils should not be used, as they do not work as well.

Culpeper says of Jasmine, 'Jasmine is a warm, cordial plant . . . it warms the womb, and heals Schirrti therein, and facilitates the birth'.

Jasmine has been used in love potions throughout the ages, so it is lucky that it can be used for the treatment of gonorrhoea. As this oil has aphrodisiac qualities; it can be used to treat frigidity, impotence and premature ejaculation.

This oil has a marked effect on the female reproductive system. It helps to relieve the pain in childbirth, and also speeds delivery and strengthens the contractions. Jasmine should be massaged over the abdomen and the lower back during labour. It is also a hormone balancer, and is therefore useful for preventing and treating postnatal depression.

Jasmine oil also helps with the flow of breast milk, and is extremely useful where this is insufficient.

'Jasmine produces a feeling of optimism, confidence and euphoria. It is most useful in cases of apathy, indifference or listlessness' (Tisserand).

Uses: Frigidity, labour pains, depression, nervous exhaustion, production of breast milk, postnatal depression.

Cautions: Not to be used just before the expected day of delivery. Its narcotic properties could disturb concentration. As this is a very strong oil only use as 1% dilution. If used when pregnant it may cause premature labour.

JUNIPER (*Juniperus communis*)
EXTRACTION is from steam distillation from the berries.

Juniper was used as incense by early civilisations. In Tibet it was used for medicinal and for religious purposes. In Rome, Arabia and Greece it was valued for its antiseptic qualities. In Mongolia the women were given Juniper berries at the onset of labour.

Culpeper says of Juniper 'the berries stay all fluxes, help haemorrhoids or piles, and kills worms in children. Juniper was one of the many herbs used to get rid of evil spirits and to ward off the plague and other contagious diseases.

In Yugoslavia oil from the berries was a cure-all for typhoid, dysentery, cholera, worms and other diseases that are brought on by poverty. Juniper berries are also used to make gin. (Perhaps that is why, in bygone days, gin was used to help procure abortions.) This oil was first distilled by Schnellenberg in 1546.

Uses: During labour, varicose veins, haemorrhoids.

Cautions: This oil is best avoided during pregnancy, if there are any kidney problems, or if being treated for cancer.

LAVENDER (*Lavendula officinale or Lavendula angustafolia*)
EXTRACTION is from steam distillation of the fresh flowering tops.

This is the most useful and most widely used of all the oils. In Arabic medicine it was used as an expectorant and an anti-spasmodic. The Romans probably introduced this plant to Britain.

Lavender's name is derived from the Latin word 'lavare' to wash. This is probably because it was used to cleanse wounds. In Roman times it was used as a perfume and for flavouring foods. In modern times it is used as a flavouring for drugs and as a nervene to treat the nervous system. Lavender was one of the Roman's favourites. They used it for bathing.

Women have been using lavender water since Elizabethan and Stuart times. It has been a favourite of women throughout the ages.

Lavender oil is very useful for childbirth. As Tisserand says 'It makes for a speedy delivery without increasing the severity of the contractions'. Culpeper says of Lavender 'It strengthens the stomach, freeth the liver and spleen from obstructions, provoketh the woman's courses and expelleth the afterbirth'.

Because of its qualities for inducing sleep it is put inside pillows. Lavender bags have been put into clothing draws and linen chests throughout the ages to keep the clothes and linen fresh and free from moths. Children used to wear lavender bags around their necks to keep them free from infections and illnesses.

Lavender is a balancer. It balances both mind and body. It is also a wonderful healer of minor burns.

Uses: Boils, bruises, burns, eczema, bites, stings, wounds, during labour, hypertension, insomnia, migraine, nervous tension, stress related conditions. It is particularly good for using in baths post natally as it relieves painful perineii and reduces the oedema and bruising. Lavender oil may be put neat onto perineal bruising as this reduces the bruising considerably and relieves the pain dramatically.

Cautions: Lavender should not be used during the first three months of pregnancy. It can also cause people with low blood pressure to feel a little slow or drowsy after use as it lowers the blood pressure.

LEMON (*Citrus limon*)

EXTRACTION of this oil is by expression from the outer part of the fresh peel.

The lemon tree is thought to have originated in Asia and introduced into Europe by the Crusaders when they discovered the lemon tree in Palestine. In historic times it had immense value as an antiseptic to be used on bites from disease carrying insects. The Egyptians used it to cure meat and fish poisoning. Lemons and Limes used to be carried on English ships to prevent scurvy, as they have a high vitamin C content. Both expressed and distilled oils of lemon were sold in Paris as early as 1692. Jean Valnet mentioned that lemon oil may be used to cure syphilis and gonorrhoea.

Uses: Anaemia, brittle nails, chilblains, cold sores, insect bites, varicose veins, high blood pressure, poor circulation, colds and helping to improve the immune system.

Cautions: This oil may cause dermal irritation or sensitisation in some individuals. It should be used in low concentration and not used on skin exposed to sunlight.

MANDARIN (*Citrus reticulata*)

EXTRACTION is by cold expression of the outer rind of the fresh peel.

The mandarin probably originated in China. It got its name as it was possibly offered to the mandarins. This oil is very gentle and is safe to use in pregnancy and for children. It is probably the gentlest of all the oils.

Uses: Stretch marks, fluid retention, digestive problems, insomnia, nausea, nervous tension. It is both antiviral and relaxing.

MARIGOLD (*Calendula officinalis*)

EXTRACTION: This oil is obtained by maceration of the petals.

Marigolds are found throughout the world in gardens. This plant is also one of the most useful herbal remedies and has been used in Arabic, Greek and Indian medicine. In Russia its nickname is Russian penicillin.

Unfortunately this oil is only produced in very small quantities and is therefore difficult to obtain.

The flowers and leaves of the marigold have been valued through the ages for their range of action. They are antiseptic and good for healing wounds, cracked nipples, varicose veins, nappy rashes, haemorrhoids, bruises, perineii, inflammation and stretch marks. It can also be used to treat anxiety and tension. Calendula is also antifungicidal.

Uses: Antiseptic, wounds, cracked nipples, varicose veins, nappy rashes, haemorrhoids, bruises, sore tail ends after delivery, inflammation and stretch marks.

MARJORAM (SWEET) (*Origanum marjoram*)

EXTRACTION is by steam distillation from the flowering dried herb.

The Latin name for marjoram is derived from major as it was thought in ancient times to confer longevity. The Greek name 'origanus' means 'joy of the mountain' and it was given to newlyweds to bring them good luck. It is still sold in Greek markets as ditany (a tea to aid digestion).

In the 17th Century Culpeper said 'it's well known being an inhabitant in every garden'. Marjoram is warming on both mind and body. It is particularly good when combined with Lavender at bedtime. As Marjoram lessens the emotional response and physical sensation it was often used in religious institutions where celibacy was essential. Marjoram was also planted in graveyards to bring peace to the departed spirits.

Uses: Bruises, high blood pressure and insomnia, 'after pains'.

Caution: Marjoram oil should not be used during pregnancy. Only to be used in the post-natal period.

NEROLI (*Citrus aurentium var amara*)

EXTRACTION: Essential oil is produced by steam distillation of the freshly picked flowers. A concrete and an absolute are produced by solvent extraction from the freshly picked flowers.

Neroli takes its name from an Italian princess (Anne-Marie, Countess of Neroli) who used it as her favourite perfume. This oil is obtained from the flower of the bitter orange. It is thought that orange trees came to Europe from the East Indies. Neroli is a very expensive oil as it takes many flowers to make just a small quantity of this oil.

The petals were used in China for making cosmetics. The Victorians put it in the eau de cologne which they used when they had an attack of the vapours. Neroli, also known as orange blossom, has been associated with weddings and marriage.

Uses: Soothing, frigidity, stretch marks (both the treatment and the prevention of), postnatal depression, palpitation and poor circulation.

NEROLI ... THE VICTORIANS USED IT IN THE EAU DE COLOGNE THAT THEY USED WHEN THEY HAD AN ATTACK OF THE VAPOURS...

PEPPERMINT (*Mentha piperita*)

EXTRACTION is by steam distillation of the flowering plant.

The Romans introduced this oil to Britain. Peppermint was familiar to Shakespeare and Chaucer. This is one of the most widely used herbs in the western world. The Romans and the Egyptians used peppermint. It was mentioned that the Pharisees in the Bible were paid in 'tithes of mint anise and cumin'. Peppermint tea is widely used as a tisane and can be used for morning sickness and heartburn. Cold compresses can be applied to the forehead to relieve headaches.

Culpeper says of peppermint 'It is food in fomentations to disperse curdled milk in the breasts.' It can be used to treat mastitis.

Uses: Colic, nausea, headaches, mastitis.

Cautions: Do not use over long periods as it could cause disturbances in sleep patterns. Peppermint should not be used at night as it tends to wake you up and therefore can cause insomnia. Do not store near homeopathic remedies as it may act as an antidote to them.

PATCHOULI (*Postegonon patchouli*)

EXTRACTION is by steam distillation of the dried leaves.

Patchouli comes from Malaysia and south-east Asia. This oil is 'very earthy' and is reminiscent of the sixties because it was used by the hippies and the flower people of that era. It has a long history of use in traditional medicine in China. And is also supposed to have aphrodisiac qualities (but that depends whether both partners like the smell or not!). It has an earthy smell that many people find unpleasant. This oil is unusual in as much as it improves with age.

Uses: Acne, dry skin, wounds, stress related conditions.

Cautions: It tends to be an appetite suppressant, which is fine if the appetite needs to be suppressed. Also it is sedative in low doses but high doses may have the opposite effect.

PETITGRAIN (*Citrus aurentium var amara*)
EXTRACTION is by steam distillation of the leaves and the young twig tips.

Another name for Petitgrain is 'poor man's neroli'. It also comes from the bitter orange tree but unlike neroli, which is distilled from the flowers, Petitgrain is obtained by distilling the leaves and young tips of the twigs. However in times gone by it was extracted from the unripe oranges, which were still green and the size of cherries, hence its name petitgrain (small grains). Petitgrain and neroli have the same properties except that petitgrain is less sedative.

Uses are the same as Neroli.

ROSE (DAMASK) (*Rose damascena*)
ROSE (CABBAGE) (*Rosa centifolia*)
EXTRACTION is by steam or water distillation from the fresh petals.

This is the most expensive of oils and is also known as the 'Queen of Oils'. It takes one ton of rose petals to make just one ounce of oil.

The healing qualities of rose have been known since the beginning of history. French and Moroccan rose possesses narcotic properties and have the reputation of being an aphrodisiac. In Roman times Wild Rose was recommended for rabid dog bites. In Ayurvedic medicine roses were considered to be cooling and a tonic for the mind. Ayurvedic medicine is the oldest, most complete medicine. It dates back to 3000BC. It means 'the science of life'. Until the 1930s rose was used in official medicine. Rose was probably the first oil distilled by Avicenna in the 10th Century.

Rose is a very feminine oil and gives a woman positive feelings about herself. It is an excellent 'womb tonic' and can be used to regulate menstruation and can help where there have been repeated miscarriages.

Rose releases the ('happy hormone') neuro-transmitter dopamine and soothes underlying tension. It is very helpful in treating sexual difficulties, frigidity and impotence in both men and women and is especially useful in increasing sperm production in men. It is also extremely useful for treating postnatal depression.

Because rose oil is so expensive, adulteration is common, therefore you should only use the best quality oil.

Uses: Insomnia, aphrodisiac, tension, postnatal depression.

Caution: It is best to avoid using this oil during pregnancy. This oil should only be used post natal.

... ROSE RELEASES THE "HAPPY HORMONE" DOPAMINE AND SOOTHES UNDERLYING TENSION ...

SAGE (*Salvia officinalis*)

EXTRACTION: Essential oils are obtained by steam distillation of the dried leaves.

The Romans called sage the miracle plant. In Latin 'salvare' means heal or save. To the Chinese it was so valuable that they exchanged two cases of tea for each case of sage. Sage originates from the Mediterranean area and has always been used for flavouring for cooking and in the brewing of ale. It has been used in folk medicine as tea, gargles and poultices.

Sage has a marked action on the female reproductive system. It was used for regulating menstruation and helping in childbirth.

John Gerard said 'Sage is particularly good for the head and the brain. It quickeneth the sense and memory', therefore wise men were called sages. It was also used by the village wise women who were burnt as witches in the 13th to 17th centuries.

Sage was also believed to assuage grief and Samuel Pepys noted in his diary that sage was planted on graves in country graveyards.

Uses: There are no uses for Sage during pregnancy, it has been added for completeness. Clary Sage is used instead of Sage.

Cautions: Sage can be toxic. This is why we use Clary Sage which has less thujone in it. It should be avoided during pregnancy. It should also be avoided if breast feeding as it can inhibit the production of breast milk.

SANDALWOOD (*Santalum album*)

EXTRACTION is by water and steam distillation.

Sandalwood trees are nearly extinct and are now only used for producing oils. Sandalwood oil has been used for many centuries in India, both as incense and in traditional medicine. It is a very powerful urinary disinfectant and can be used for treating the whole of the urinary tract.

Sandalwood has been used for more than two and a half thousand years. It is very popular as a perfume and has aphrodisiac qualities, but unlike the other aphrodisiacs it actually lives up to its expectations. Luckily it can also be used to treat gonorrhoea. This oil is very efficient against the streptococcus and the staphylococcus aureus, which is why it can be used for the treatment of sore throats.

Uses: Dry and cracked skin, cystitis, insomnia, aphrodisiac.

Caution: Do not use excessively if you are epileptic.

TEA TREE (*Melaleuca alternafolia*)

EXTRACTION is by steam or water distillation of the leaves and twigs.

The Tea Tree has no relationship to the tea that we drink. This oil is one of the only two oils which can be used neat. Tea Tree is an important oil as it is antifungal, antiviral, antiseptic and antibacterial. It is also a very important imuno-activator and increases the body's ability to respond to infection. Tea Tree can be put neat on cold sores (or added to a few drops of vodka if preferred). It can also be used in the treatment of thrush and it has been used by some therapists for the treatment of patients with AIDS (no papers have been published as yet).

The Australian Aborigines used the Tea Tree to dress infected wounds and when the English settlers couldn't get medical supplies they followed suit. During the Second World War it was included in the medical supplies for troops in the tropics.

Uses: Cold sores, thrush, cystitis, nappy rash.

Caution: In some people this oil may cause irritation.

YLANG YLANG (*Cananga odorata*)

EXTRACTION is by water or steam distillation from the fresh flowers.

Ylang Ylang comes from the cananga odorata tree which grows in Java, the Philippines, Sumatra, and Madagascar. The best oils come from the flowers that are picked in the early morning in the summer. It is very sweet and sickly and is best used with a citrus oil such as Lemon or Bergamot as this offsets the sweetness.

Ylang Ylang is hypotensive and reduces tachycardia and hyperpnoea. It can be used to calm fear and anxiety. It is both calming and relaxing, which is why it can also be used as an aphrodisiac. In Indonesia the flowers are spread on the marriage beds of newly married couples on their wedding night.

YLANG YLANG – IN INDONESIA THE FLOWERS ARE SPREAD ON THE MARRIAGE BEDS OF NEWLY MARRIED COUPLES ON THEIR WEDDING NIGHT...

Ylang Ylang was put into macassar oil which was widely used as a hair oil by the Victorians. This is why anti-macassars were needed to protect the back of their chairs.

Uses: High blood pressure, palpitations, depression, aphrodisiac, insomnia, stress.

Caution: This oil should not be used in high concentration. 1-1½% is strong enough as used in excess its heady scent can cause nausea and headache.

3 | Pregnancy and Conditions

Aromatherapy is an holistic therapy. It treats the mind, the body and the spirit. Throughout pregnancy the baby is aware of the emotional state of the mother, and, to a degree, the external environment. Therefore the oils the mother inhales, uses in the bath or for massage are sensed by the baby.

The essential oils induce relaxation, dispel fears and anxieties, and can relieve the aches and pains caused by the relaxation of the ligaments, postural changes and extra weight. They also, with massage, help to improve the circulation, stimulate the lymphatic system, help with the elimination of toxins, as well as helping with the prevention of varicose veins and oedema.

...THROUGHOUT PREGNANCY THE BABY IS AWARE OF THE EMOTIONAL STATE OF THE MOTHER...

There are a small group of oils that should not be used during the first three months of pregnancy either because they are emmenogogues (they encourage menstruation) or because they can be toxic. *Oils that are recommended for labour should not be used during pregnancy as they can encourage premature labour*.

When massaging during pregnancy be gentle, especially over the abdomen and the lower back.

Conditions that may occur during pregnancy, labour or post natal and recommended essential oils

BRUISES: Lavender, Fennel, Geranium, Marigold, Sweet Marjoram.

BURNS: Lavender, Marigold, Chamomile.

CHAPPED AND CRACKED SKIN: Patchouli, Sandalwood.

COLD SORES: Tea Tree, Lemon.

CRACKED NIPPLES: Lavender, Marigold, Roman Chamomile, Frankincense.

CUTS: Lavender, Marigold.

ENGORGED BREASTS: Geranium, Peppermint.

HAEMORRHOIDS: Cypress, Geranium, Juniper.

HEADACHES: Peppermint, Lavender.

HIGH BLOOD PRESSURE: Lavender, Roman Chamomile, Lemon, Neroli, Ylang Ylang.

INFECTIONS: Tea Tree, Lemon.

INSOMNIA: Lavender, Roman Chamomile, Mandarin, Tangerine.

INSUFFICIENT MILK: Fennel, Jasmine.

LABOUR: Jasmine, Lavender, Clary Sage, Cinnamon.

MASTITIS: Peppermint.

OEDEMA: Geranium, Cypress, Lavender, Patchouli.

POSTNATAL DEPRESSION: Jasmine, Rose, Neroli.

INSECT BITES: Lavender, Tea Tee, Chamomile, Lemon, Marigold.

STRETCH MARKS: Neroli, Tangerine, Mandarin.

VARICOSE VEINS: Cypress, Lemon.

Essential oils safe for pregnancy after the first three months

Chamomile	Mandarin
Cypress	Marigold
Eucalyptus	Peppermint
Frankincense	Sandalwood
Lavender (with caution)	Tea Tree
Lemon	Ylang Ylang

Essential oils for labour

Cinnamon	Jasmine
Clary Sage	Lavender
Chamomile	

Essential oils for post natal period

Chamomile	Geranium	Peppermint
Clary Sage	Jasmine	Petitgrain
Cypress	Lavender	Rose
Eucalyptus	Lemon	Sandalwood
Fennel	Marigold	Tea Tree
Frankincense	Neroli	Ylang Ylang

Essential oils to avoid during pregnancy

Angelica	Fennel	Origanum
Aniseed	Hyssop	Parsley
Arnica	Jasmine	Rosemary
Basil	Juniper	Rose
Camphor	Lovage	Sage
Cedarwood	Melissa	Sweet Marjoram
Clary Sage	Myrrh	Tarragon
Clove	Marjoram	Thyme
Cinnamon		

4 | Recipes

Bites and Stings
Put on the bite 1 drop of Lavender or 1 drop of Tea Tree. If the insect has left its sting in remove it carefully with some tweezers first.

Burns
Put the burnt area under the cold tap for 5 minutes, then put on the burn 1 drop of Lavender oil. *If it is a large burnt area you should go to Casualty.*

Colds
If you feel a cold or sore throat coming on put 1 drop of Tea Tree oil each side of the throat and 1 drop on the bridge of the nose. Hopefully it will improve your immune system and stop the cold from developing.

Cold Sores
Put 1 drop of Tea Tree oil on the end of a cotton wool bud and then put it on the sore. *Cold sores are highly contagious* so don't kiss your baby. Wash your hands after touching the sore.

Flu
Put 2-3 drops of Tea Tree or Eucalyptus oil in an oil burner. Do not let the reservoir burn dry. *If you are ill and pregnant contact your doctor or midwife.*

Haemorrhoids
Unfortunately this inconvenient, uncomfortable condition is very common during pregnancy due to the pressure of the uterus and the relaxation of the semilunar valves in the veins due to the increased levels of progesterone. The following oils can be used in a sitz bath or as a compress: Cypress, Geranium, Frankincense. (See dilution methods page 15).

Headaches

A cold compress of Lavender or 1 drop of Lavender massaged neat into the temples. A cold compress of Peppermint to the temples or forehead, but not at night as it tends to wake you up. 1 drop of Lavender and 2 drops of Marjoram added to 1 tablespoon of base oil sprinkled in the bath water can also be used.

Hypertension (high blood pressure)

Either add 6 drops of the following diluted oils to the bath water as above or use as a massage oil avoiding the abdomen and lower back: Roman Chamomile, Lavender, Lemon, Ylang Ylang, Neroli.

Insomnia

This condition is very common during pregnancy, especially if it is difficult to get comfortable at night. Also at night, when all is quiet a conflict of emotions can rear its ugly head. 1–2 drops of Lavender can be put on the pillow at night.

A bath containing not more than 6 drops of one or two of the following oils added to the bath water can be used: Roman Chamomile, Lavender, Mandarin, Tangerine.

Mood Swings and Emotional Upsets

With pregnancy comes a flood of conflicting emotions: 'Do I still look attractive?;' 'Labour and the fear of it'; 'How painful will it be?'; 'Can I cope with it?'; 'How can I cope with a baby?'; 'What are the financial implications?' The hormone changes don't help.

One of the following oils added to a bath will help restore self-confidence, lift the depression and raise the spirits: Put 6 drops in a base oil before adding it to the bath full or water: Geranium, Neroli.

Oedema (Swelling)

This is very common during pregnancy especially during hot weather or if you are on your feet a lot. However do not ignore this condition. If you have swelling you should check with your doctor or midwife that there is no problem.

In 2 teaspoonsful of carrier oil choose 4 drops of one of the following: Geranium, Cypress, Lavender, Patchouli. Massage from the ankles, moving upwards with long strokes. This will reduce the swelling. Do not massage over varicose veins.

Stretch Marks
As prevention is better than cure massage one of the following oils into the abdomen gently daily. In 2 teaspoonsful of carrier oil: Tangerine, Mandarin, Neroli.

Vaginal Thrush
Add 4 drops of Tea Tree oil to a bowl of warm water and sit in it for 5 to 10 minutes.

5 | Labour

The value of massage with aromatic herbs have been known for centuries. Many hospitals are now accepting aromatherapy as an alternative method of analgesia. Some oils (e.g. Jasmine or Lavender) can relieve the pain of the contractions and can help give strong, efficient contractions which help to shorten labour. These oils can also help with the expulsion of the placenta.

Nicholas Culpeper's *Directory for Midwives* said 'if travail be hard anoint the belly with oyl of Sweet Almonds, Lilies and Sweet oil.'

Pain relief in labour

In early labour 2–3 drops of Jasmine or Lavender may be used in a burner, though it is probably not a good idea in a maternity unit because of the gases (e.g. oxygen), and you may well set off the smoke alarms or sprinkler systems.

In a bath full of water add 8–10 drops of Lavender oil or 4–5 drops of Jasmine oil in 2 teaspoonsful of base oil. Or 6–8 drops of Clary Sage in 2 teaspoonsful of base oil.

The following oils can be used for massage over the back or lower abdomen. They are analgesic and can help give regular, efficient contractions. In 30mls of base oil add one of the following: 7 drops Jasmine oil or 14 drops of Lavender oil or 10 drops of Clary Sage or 10 drops of Cinnamon oil.

Exhaustion in labour

Your labour may go on longer than you thought and you may become tired. The following method will help to revive you.

Body Sponging: Mix 2–3 drops of Mandarin essential oil in ½ teaspoon of base oil. Add this to a bowl of cool water and ask your partner to sponge you with it. Avoid contact with the eyes.

Do not use essential oils in the water if you are having a water birth as the oils could possibly come into contact with the baby's eyes.

... ADD THIS TO A BOWL OF COOL WATER AND ASK YOUR PARTNER TO SPONGE YOU WITH IT...

6 | Post natal

Breast engorgement

About three or four days post-natally the breasts become very full and engorged. The body tends to go into overdrive with the milk production until it realises how much is actually needed.

Breasts become larger, heavier, tender and need handling with care. This is reduced as the baby suckles. Peppermint oil in a cold compress is probably the safest if the mother is still breast feeding. Other oils may be used but only in 1% dilution. Geranium oil in a compress or 6 drops in a base oil in a bath full of water.

Cabbage leaves, washed thoroughly and dried, with the hard green stalks removed, applied to the breasts, as a poultice will reduce the inflammation. Unless you want to dry up the milk only leave them on for one hour to an hour and a half. They are very soothing and take away the pain and discomfort. If they cause itching and irritation – as can very occasionally happen – remove them at once.

To increase lactation

A number of plants have been known for centuries to promote the flow of breast milk and have been used as herbal teas and infusions. In Aromatherapy the following oils are recommended – Fennel: 7 drops of Fennel oil to 25mls of carrier oil; or Jasmine: 7 drops of Jasmine oil to 25mls of carrier oil. Massage from the top of the breast to the nipple using either of the top two oils. *Caution: wash the breasts before feeding the baby.*

Mastitis

Use a cold compress of Peppermint oil. Cabbage leaves washed and dried thoroughly and applied to the affected areas will help to relieve the pain and discomfort and bring down the inflammation. Only leave on for an hour to an hour and a half at a time or you will suppress lactation.

Cracked Nipples

Lavender oil, Roman Chamomile oil, Frankincense oil or Calendula oil.

One drop of essential oil to 1 teaspoonful of vegetable oil (not a nut based carrier oil). Apply to the nipple after feeding. This should be washed off the nipple before the next feed. Careful, correct fixing of the baby should help to prevent cracked nipples. The nipples should be exposed to the air between feeds.

Geranium leaves placed on the nipples furry side helps to heal cracked nipples. They are just the right shape for the nipples. Geranium leaves also help to relieve the pain and discomfort of cracked nipples. They tingle. Remove the leaves if they cause itching or irritation.

Muscular tension in the shoulders

This is usually caused by poor posture when feeding your baby. Before you start make sure that you are sitting comfortably. Have your back supported and put your feet up on a pouffe or a coffee table, or sit on a low chair. Remember you may have to be sitting there for 20–30 minutes, so you might as well be comfy. Feeding your baby should be an enjoyable experience – if you are uncomfortable it won't be. Anyway you should make the most of any opportunity to rest that comes your way, you're going to need it!

...BEFORE YOU START MAKE SURE THAT YOU ARE SITTING COMFORTABLY...

Perineum (bruised and painful)

Neat Lavender may be put directly onto the bruised area. 8-10 drops of Lavender oil in a bath of water. 8-10 drops of Calendula in 1 tablespoon of base oil in a bath of water. Lavender oil is the best oil to use for this and will give pain relief almost immediately. Lavender oil will also help boost the immune system and fight infection.

Infected Perineum

A bath of water containing 5 drops of Tea Tree oil and 5 drops of Lavender oil.

Compresses of Tea Tree and Lavender.

In a bowl of warm water put 4 drops of Tea Tree, mix well and sit in it for 5-10 minutes.

Sticky Caesarian Section wounds

Bathe and compress as above.

Post Natal Depression

There are many essential oils which can be used post natally to banish baby blues, balance the emotions and help with mood swings. Jasmine is probably one of the best. 6-8 drops of Jasmine oil in 1 tablespoon of base oil in a bath of water. The following oils may also be used: Neroli, Rose, Mandarin, Tangerine.

A full massage may also be given using any of the above oils. If using Jasmine, Rose or Neroli use 5-6 drops in 25mls of base oil. If using the other oils use 10-12 drops in 25mls of base oil.

7 | The New Baby

Essential oils can be used beneficially on the new baby. Regular treatment can boost the immune system thus resulting in fewer colds and infections.

Roman Chamomile is known as the children's oil since it is gentle, safe and low in toxicity. German Chamomile, Lavender, Tangerine and Mandarin are also very gentle. Tea Tree and Eucalyptus can also be used in burners for colds.

Bathing

Always dilute essential oils with a teaspoonful of carrier oil when bathing a baby as globules of essential oil will remain on the surface of the bath water and perhaps get into the baby's eyes, nose or mouth via splashes or the baby's hands. *Do not be tempted to add extra drops of oil for luck.*

Babies 0-2 months: 1 drop per 15mls carrier oil for massage.
Babies 0-2 months: 1 drop per teaspoonful carrier oil for baths.

Baby Massage

A baby needs to be held and to be touched. Touch is one of the first senses to which your baby will respond. By massaging your baby he will sense your love and respond positively. It has been shown that babies who are handled often become more aware and respond more to their surroundings. They will also become more aware of the position of their limbs as well as feeling more loved and more relaxed. By massaging your baby you will get to know him/her, build up your self-confidence in your ability to handle him/her and will communicate messages of love and reassurance.

Choose a time to massage your baby when he/she is not hungry or over-tired. Allow yourself plenty of time as massage should never be rushed. Do not massage straight after you have fed him/her as baby will need to digest the feed.

. . . TAKE THE PHONE OFF THE HOOK TO AVOID INTERRUPTIONS . . .

Before you start to massage your baby unplug the phone and put a 'do not disturb' note on the front door as that is probably the time that people will decide to ring or call.

Contraindications
Wait until the baby's six to eight week assessment.

If the baby has brittle bone disease under no circumstances massage.

If the baby is unwell.

Right after vaccination.

If the baby is on medication.

If the baby or you have any skin infection.

If the baby has any infection or skin problems check with your GP first.

Which oils to use?
Roman Chamomile oil is well known as the children's oil as it has very low toxicity and is extremely safe and gentle. Other oils which can be used are German Chamomile, Lavender, Mandarin, Tangerine and Rose. As a carrier oil I would use light Coconut oil.

How much oil to use?

Babies 0-2 months: 1 drop per 15mls (3 teaspoonsful).

Babies 2-12 months: 1 drop per 10mls (2 teaspoonsful).

The room should be warm (24-26°C or 75-80°F), draught-free, away from distracting stimuli and bright lights. There should be plenty of room for movement. Take the phone off the hook to avoid interruptions. A relaxed atmosphere can be created by playing some soothing background music. Choose a comfortable position (probably the floor is the safest) and place the baby on a blanket or quilt covered by a towel. Make sure that you are comfortable, and take care with your posture or you may get backache.

Before you start make sure that your nails are not long and jagged, and remove watches and jewellery as you can scratch your baby. Wash your hands and strip your baby leaving a nappy under him in case of accidents. Place your massage oil in a bowl where you can easily reach it and where he can't. Make sure that your hands are warm.

The length of time spent on massaging your baby will depend on your baby and his mood. Start initially with 5-10 minutes and then progress according to the situation. If your baby gets upset as sometimes happens with the first massage then stop the massage, wrap him up and cuddle him. Toddlers often enjoy a massage and when feeling tired, irritable and stressed may ask for one. A massage may help to introduce a quiet period in an otherwise hectic day.

Massaging your baby will also improve his circulation, decrease tension (both maternal and infant), decrease stress and irritability, help with bonding, and hopefully he will sleep better. Massaging your baby may also help to improve his immune system. Massage helps the baby's skin to eliminate toxins and waste products. It also aids digestion and relieves colic and constipation.

Techniques

Normally do 4-6 repetitions with each stroke. Use a firm but gentle stroke to avoid tickling him/her. Use a sweeping motion. Be careful when picking the baby up after the massage as he/she will be slippery.

Chest and Stomach

1. Starting with both hands together at the centre of the chest, gently push out to the sides of the ribs. Then, without removing your hands from the baby bring them back to the centre in a heart-shaped movement.

2. From the tip of the breast bone gently and firmly, using the pads of your thumbs, fill the whole chest with circular movements. Work up the chest and out over the collarbone, ending with a long stroke down the arms.

3. Make sure you have plenty of oil on your hands, and taking care not to press too heavily, with the heel of the massaging hand over the pubic bone, fanning your fingers out, make a gentle sweeping movement from left to right.

4. Oil your hands again, and using the pads of your index and middle fingers fill in the abdomen with tiny circles, starting with the bottom of the right hand side and up in an arc, ending at the base of the left side of the abdomen (a large semi-circle working clockwise).

5. Next finish with a few fan movements (as above).

Arms

1. Do one arm at a time. First oil the arms.

2. Support the lower arm with one hand, firmly and gently.

3. Use firm, gentle circles with the pads of your thumb and massage the upper arm from elbow to armpit. Fill in the whole upper arm with these circles.

4. Next, repeat the same for the lower arm. Use your thumb and index finger to open the hands gently and massage the fingers.

5. After this gently but firmly do a long sweeping stroke from wrist to shoulders.

Legs

1. As for the arms, the legs are done one at a time. They are similar to the arms.

2. First oil the legs.

3. Supporting the leg, work in thumb circles from the knee to the hip and groin, working all the way round. Next work from the ankle to the knee. Then draw little semicircles on the knee. Support the foot by gently cradling the heel and lower leg in one hand.

4. With the other hand, using the thumb, very gently massage the feet. Finish with a long sweeping stroke up the legs from ankle to hip and over hip.

Back

1. Oil the back and buttocks using long sweeping strokes.

2. Massage each buttock using thumb or finger circles, working up towards the spine and waist until the whole buttocks have been filled in.

3. Next do long sweeping strokes up the whole half of the back to the shoulder, out down the arms and through the fingers. Do not massage down the baby's spine.

4. Using tiny thumb circles, taking care not to press too hard, work up each side of the spine. Fill in the whole of the back with this movement.

5. Finish off with the long sweeping stroke.

Minor Hiccoughs or the Harsh Realities!

Hiccoughs: Ignore hiccoughs as they don't worry the baby. He/she had them before he/she was born.

Colic: 1 drop of Roman Chamomile to 1 teaspoonful of carrier oil. Gently rub abdomen, back and feet. If breast feeding check your diet. Wine, citrus fruit, grapes, or fried onions maybe the main culprits.

Cradle Cap: 1 drop of Geranium oil to 1 teaspoonful of carrier oil. Gently massage into the scalp.

Coughs and colds: Eucalyptus or Tea Tree may be used in a burner.

Insomnia and restlessness: Lavender or Roman Chamomile may be used in a burner (don't let the reservoir burn dry). 1 drop of Lavender or Roman Chamomile on a cotton wool ball placed at the foot of the cot. If it is placed at the top of the cot the baby may well get it on his hands and from there into his eyes or mouth.

Nappy Rash: Wash the nappy area in a bowl of warm water with either 1 drop of Roman Chamomile or 1 drop of Lavender oil in order to prevent nappy rash. If your baby develops nappy rash add 3 drops of Lavender oil and 3 drops of Roman Chamomile to a 100g jar of zinc and castor oil cream or Chamomile ointment. Mix well. This should only be used if the need arises.

8 | Last but not least . . . don't forget Dad

Let us give a thought to the person without whom none of this would be possible – Dad. How does he feel? Excited perhaps as there's going to be a replica of himself. Afraid perhaps because now he is going to have another mouth to feed, and perhaps may have to manage on just one salary. Jealous perhaps because now his work is done you may love your baby more than him, or perhaps instead of putting his needs first there is

...LET US GIVE A THOUGHT TO THE PERSON WITHOUT WHOM NONE OF THIS WOULD BE POSSIBLE...

someone else to consider. He may even be confused. Up to now you have been able to cope with most things, in fact you were a veritable superwoman. Now your brain has turned to cotton wool and you're putting the dinner in the fridge and the milk in the oven. Maybe he is having to cope with mood changes. One minute you're all sweetness and light, next you are attacking him with claws unsheathed. Hormones are difficult things for most men to understand. A small shift in your hormone levels can mean a big shift in your moods and emotions. It can mean the difference of being able to cope or not with the world around you.

Common Problems

Insomnia

Perhaps he is worried about how he is going to cope financially or emotionally or indeed if he's ready for fatherhood. It probably doesn't help that you are tossing and turning unable to get comfortable or sleep or that you have to make several trips to the loo at night. Put 1-2 drops of Lavender on his pillow at night. A bath containing 6-8 drops of one or two of the following essential oils in 1 teaspoon of base oil to a full bath of water: Chamomile; Lavender; Neroli; Sandalwood.

Lack of Libido

This is a very common problem. If you have gone off sex too there is no problem. This is probably because you are changing shape, or he may be afraid of hurting you or the baby. Maybe he feels that there is very little point as his job's done. Perhaps he feels a little insecure. Cuddles are just as important as sex.

Try a body massage with: 4 drops of Neroli in 4 teaspoons of base oil; 8 drops of Sandalwood to 4 teaspoons of base oil; 4 drops of Ylang Ylang in 4 teaspoons of base oil.

Stress or Tension

In a full bath of water use 6-8 drops of one or two of the following oils in one teaspoon of base oil: Neroli; Patchouli; Sandalwood; Tangerine. Or you could try a full body massage using any of the above oils. Don't use more than two oils together at any one time and make sure that if you are using more than one oil at a time that they smell good together. *Do not use more than 6-8 drops of essential oil in 4 teaspoons of base oil.*

...CUDDLES ARE JUST AS IMPORTANT AS SEX...

9 | Case Studies

One – Chris was a 28 years old sales assistant, having her second baby. Her son, Mark was six years old. She lived with her boyfriend, Luke. Chris had a phobia about hospitals as 'people went there to die'. Just thinking about hospitals gave her panic attacks. She opted for a home confinement.

Mark, her son was a breech delivery, induced at 41 weeks. He was a spontaneous breech delivery and weighed 7lbs 15ozs. Labour only lasted 6 hours. Whilst she was pregnant with Mark, Chris was taken into hospital with raised blood pressure. Her mother suffers from high blood pressure. Chris does not smoke or drink alcohol.

At 19 weeks of pregnancy she had a routine scan which confirmed her dates, but she had to make several attempts to get to the hospital and had several missed appointments, such was her fear of hospitals. When she actually reached the hospital she was in tears and was shaking uncontrollably.

Chris's blood pressure at booking was 120/80. At 30 weeks pregnancy her blood pressure climbed to 140/100 and she had oedema (swelling) of the hands and feet. Chris did not want to go to hospital in spite of the dangers being explained so I rang the hospital and talked to the consultant and explained the situation. He said that she could stay at home as long as she remained asymptomatic and the diastole (the lower blood pressure) was under /105. He said that he thought it was unlikely that she would remain out of hospital for her entire pregnancy. Chris said that she would like to try aromatherapy.

For the first three weeks we tried 6-8 drops of Lavender in her bath water and took her blood pressure and tested her urine daily. Towards the end of the first week her blood pressure settled to 130/78-120/78. After the first week we took the blood pressure alternate days. It remained within those two limits. The Lavender also improved her sleep.

Week four we decided to change to Ylang Ylang oil as we did not want to over use the Lavender. Chris complained that she wasn't sleeping as well and that she was 'feeling randy'. She had discovered the aphrodisiac qualities of that oil. Her blood pressure remained normal. Week five and week six we used Lavender with a good result. Week seven we used Roman Chamomile with good results. The sleep problem was resolved.

In the 38th week of pregnancy Chris started to get some mild contractions. She was in early labour. Her blood pressure was stable. Two hours later she had a very heavy vaginal bleed. She did not want to go to hospital in spite of the dangers being explained to her. It took another two hours to persuade her that in this circumstance perhaps the hospital was the safest place so she was persuaded to go. Chris progressed quickly to a normal delivery of a beautiful 5lb 8oz little girl. Mum and baby went home 4 hours later. The cause of the bleeding was never discovered.

Unfortunately, since her admission to hospital and coming home, she suffered from nightmares and panic attacks. She was also waking up in the middle of the night drenched in cold sweats and shaking uncontrollably. 8-10 drops of Lavender oil in her bath water helped her to sleep and reduced the panic attacks dramatically.

Two – Jane was having her first baby at home. She was 31 years old and was very adamant about what she wanted. Under no circumstance did she want any drugs, any interference or to go to hospital. She knew exactly what she wanted and nothing would make her change her mind.

At 40 weeks, on her exact due date, she went into labour and progressed well until her cervix was 6cms dilated. That took about three hours. The contractions stopped and four hours later there had been no advance. Jane did not want her 'waters broken' to get her restarted or to go to hospital (we have certain criteria we have to follow). Four hours later her cervix had only progressed to 7cms dilatation. Her contractions were weak and irregular now. She was very tired but would still not entertain any interference. However she was willing to use some Lavender oil that she had in the house.

We mixed 2 drops of Lavender oil in 2 teaspoonsful of Sunflower oil and massaged it onto her lower back and abdomen. Within 15 minutes her contractions became stronger, more regular, more efficient and less painful. Thirty minutes later her membranes ruptured and her cervix was 9cms dilated. Two hours later she had been safely delivered of a lovely, healthy 8lb 4oz boy in an excellent condition. Jane was delighted with the outcome.

Three – Katie is a full time mum with a two and a half year old daughter called Saffron. Saffron was born at home with two independent midwives. Saffron was a breech delivery. The independent midwives who delivered Saffron used Clary Sage oil. However Katie had agreed to go to hospital this time if the baby was a breech presentation (bottom or feet first). She also decided that she would like to use aromatherapy again this time as it was all the pain relief, apart from a little gas and air that she needed with Saffron.

Katie's pregnancy was uneventful and at 36 weeks we discussed which aromatherapy oils she wanted to use. We decided to try Jasmine as she had some emotional problems, she did not like being touched in labour, didn't produce enough breast milk last time, and didn't really like the smell of Clary Sage. As Katie did not like to be touched we decided to use the oil in a burner and in her bath water.

Katie went into labour at 40 weeks very slowly. At midday her cervix was 2-3cms dilated. I left her with my phone number in case she needed me and went off to do other work. She was quite happy to potter around the house with the burner on. At 4pm there was no advance so I went home, instructing her to call me when she felt that she needed me.

At 10pm the contractions were stronger and her cervix was 4cms dilated, so I stayed. At midnight I called the second midwife. Katie let us massage the Jasmine oil into her abdomen and back as it gave her more relief. (As Jasmine oil is very strong we only used one drop of Jasmine oil to two teaspoonsful of sunflower oil.)

At 2.00am Katie's cervix was 9cms dilated and she felt that she needed the gas and air.

At 2.30am Katie gave birth to a beautiful little girl weighing in at 8lbs 15ozs and named the baby 'Jasmine'. After delivery Katie mentioned that she felt 'much more loving towards her partner'.

Katie, her partner John, had a wonderful night's sleep, as did the two midwives. I usually find it extremely difficult to sleep after conducting a delivery as my adrenaline levels are still very high but that night was an exception.

Breast feeding was a complete success. Katie fed for six months without having to supplement Jasmine's feeds with bottle milk. When Saffron was born she had to supplement the feed after 2 weeks as Saffron was having weight loss.

10 | Bibliography

A Text-book of Pharmacology, G.E. Trease (1945).

A Text-book of Materia Medica, H.G. Greenish (1924).

The Encyclopaedia of Essential Oils, Julia Lawless (1992).

Directory of Essential Oils, Wanda Sellar (1992).

Culpeper's Complete Herbal and English Physician.

The Art of Aromatherapy, Robert Tisserand (1992).

A Text-book of Holistic Aromatherapy, W. Arnold Taylor (1981).

The Natural Pharmacy, Pollun and Robbins (1992).

OTHER BOOKS FROM AMBERWOOD PUBLISHING ARE:

Aromatherapy Lexicon – *The Essential Reference* by Geoff Lyth and Sue Charles is a colourful, fun way to learn about Aromatherapy. £4.99.

Aromatherapy – *The Baby Book* by Marion Del Gaudio Mak. An easy to follow guide to massage for the infant or child. £3.99

Aromatherapy – *Simply For You* by Marion Del Gaudio Mak. A clear, simple and comprehensive guide to Aromatherapy for beginners. £1.99.

Aromatherapy – *A Guide for Home Use* by Christine Westwood. All you need to know about essential oils and using them. £1.99.

Aromatherapy – *for Stress Management* by Christine Westwood. Covering the use of essential oils for everyday stress-related problems. £3.50.

Aromatherapy – *For Healthy Legs and Feet* by Christine Westwood. A guide to the use of essential oils for the treatment of legs and feet. £2.99.

Aromatherapy – *A Nurses Guide* by Ann Percival SRN. The ultimate, safe, lay guide to the natural benefits of Aromatherapy. Including recipes and massage techniques for many medical conditions and a quick reference chart. £2.99.

Aromatherapy – *A Nurses Guide for Women* by Ann Percival SRN. Concentrates on women's health for all ages. Including sections on PMT, menopause, infertility, cellulite. £2.99.

Aromatherapy – *Essential Oils in Colour* by Rosemary Caddy Bsc Hons, ARCS MISP is a unique book depicting the chemistry of essential oils. £9.99.

Aroma Science – *The Chemistry & Bioactivity of Essential Oils* by Dr Maria Lis-Balchin. With a comprehensive list of the Oils and scientific analysis. Includes sections on the sense of smell and the history of Aromatherapy. £4.99.

Plant Medicine – *A Guide for Home Use* (New Edition) by Charlotte Mitchell MNIMH. A guide to home use giving an insight into the wonderful healing qualities of plants. £2.99.

Woman Medicine – *Vitex Agnus Castus* by Simon Mills MA, FNIMH. The story of the herb that has been used for centuries in the treatment of women's problems. £2.99.

Ancient Medicine – *Ginkgo Biloba* (New Edition) by Dr Desmond Corrigan BSc(Pharms), MA, Phd, FLS, FPSI. Improved memory, circulation and concentration are associated with Ginkgo and explained in this book. £2.99.

Indian Medicine – *The Immune System* by Dr Desmond Corrigan BSc(Pharms), MA, Phd, FLS, FPSI. An intriguing account of the history of the plant called Echinacea and its power to influence the immune system. £2.99.

Herbal Medicine for Sleep & Relaxation by Dr Desmond Corrigan BSc(Pharms), MA, PhD, FLS, FPSI. A guide to the natural sedatives as an alternative to orthodox drug therapies, drawing on the latest medical research, presented in an easy reference format. £2.99.

Herbal First Aid by Andrew Chevallier BA, MNIMH. A beautifully clear reference book of natural remedies and general first aid in the home. £2.99.

Natural Taste – Herbal Teas, A Guide for Home Use by Andrew Chevallier BA, MNIMH. Contains a comprehensive compendium of Herbal Teas gives information on how to make it, its benefits, history and folklore. £3.50.

Garlic– How Garlic Protects Your Heart by Prof E. Ernst MD, PhD. Used as a medicine for over 4500 years, this book examines the latest scientific evidence supporting Garlic's effect in reducing cardiovascular disease, the Western World's number one killer. £3.99.

Phytotherapy – Fifty Vital Herbs by Andrew Chevallier, the most popular medicinal herbs with uses and advice written by an expert. £6.99

Insomnia – Doctor I Can't Sleep by Dr Adrian Williams FRCP. Written by one of the world's leading sleep experts, Dr Williams explains the phenomenon of sleep and sleeping disorders and gives advice on treatment. With 25% of the adult population reporting difficulties sleeping – this book will be essential reading for many. £2.99.

Signs & Symptoms of Vitamin Deficiency by Dr Leonard Mervyn BSc, PhD, C.Chem, FRCS. A home guide for self diagnosis which explains and assesses Vitamin Therapy for the prevention of a wide variety of diseases and illnesses. £2.99.

Causes & Prevention of Vitamin Deficiency by Dr Leonard Mervyn BSc, PhD, C.Chem, FRCS. A home guide to the Vitamin content of foods and the depletion caused by cooking, storage and processing. It includes advice for those whose needs are increased due to lifestyle, illness etc. £2.99.

Eyecare Eyewear – For Better Vision by Mark Rossi Bsc, MBCO. A complete guide to eyecare and eyewear including an assessment of the types of spectacles and contact lenses available and the latest corrective surgical procedures. £3.99.

Arthritis and Rheumatism by Dr John Cosh FRCP, MD. Covers all forms of Arthritis, its effects and the treatments available. £4.95.